How to Journal Through Tough Times

Tom Garz

Published by TG Ideas LLC, 2022.

HOW TO JOURNAL THROUGH TOUGH TIMES

First edition. November 29, 2022.

ISBN: 979-8215204931

Written by Tom Garz.

Table of Contents

This book is dedicated to YOU, the reader.

Thanks for your interest and for buying my book.

Introduction

I WAS DRIVING HOME in the fall of 2015 and little did I know that I was about to get another one of those "Life Wake Up Calls". As I was driving, I was listening to a talk program discussing one of the Presidential Candidates for the 2016 Election. I was glued to the discussions and it only got worse over the next year or so until the election. How could this happen, I thought? How could this person be President? Well, life went on, and I continued to be transfixed by the news of what was going on with our new President. Then came the Pandemic! Then came Violence with Multiple Shootings and an Assault on the White House on January 6, 2020, when we now had a new President, yet the previous President would just not give up, and it goes on even today in 2022. Then and now, we were dealing with a shaky Economy, too. Now we have rather severe Inflation that might lead to a Recession or an Economic Depression. All this time from 2015 until writing this book in 2021-2022, I was getting all wound up with the whirlwind of events. Maybe I was going into a personal depression, too, being overwhelmed with what happened, what is happening now, and probably what will happen again. I didn't do therapy at that time but rather turned to my old standby of writing my inner thoughts and feelings. Today, the term for this is journaling so I'll use that in this book. Writing equals Journaling for me. In this book, I have sorted myself out, and am sharing it with you so that maybe you can resolve your past and move on. I wish you good luck, good health, and good happiness.

As I said, in this book, I sort myself out concerning what happened between 2015 and 2022. The title of this book is "How to Journal

Through Tough Times". Maybe you have different "Tough Times" now than what I wrote in the next chapter – My Story. Maybe you're still wrestling with the topics I cover in "My Story", though. Either way, this book might help you sort yourself out – even if you can't sort others out. This book might give you a way out of where you are now. My Story gives you an example of how journaling helps me. You can do similar, if you want, in your own way with the topics that are relevant in your life.

Here's how I journal – I just sit down and write. Sometimes I sketch my thoughts or feelings. Other times, I might draw out a flow chart, a timeline, or a picture of the concepts floating around in my mind and the world around me. I don't do a fancy journal like some like to do. I just have a pen that I like and a pad of paper that I also like. In writing My Story on the computer, I was stuck writing and the words didn't come out. I learned that if I change the font to Comic Sans, instead of Arial, then I could write. I guess writing in the Arial font triggered my mind that this is "work" and my emotions stopped. Whatever way you get the words going is best for you. By the way, I'm publishing a Tough Times Journaling Workbook or something like that soon - If you can't find it, let me know, and I'll send you a link. A lot of my journaling is writing how I feel and not a litany of what's going on – but some people use journaling to just keep a record of events, like a diary – everyone is different.

Anyhow, on with the story. I've journaled in all sorts of locations – the main thing for me is to be in a place free of distractions. Distractions to me might be different to you, though. I can easily journal in a public place with "people noise" going on, as long as something or someone doesn't irritate me or distract me on a long-term basis. If the distraction is temporary, I just pause my work for a few minutes, then resume. If the distraction looks like it is here to stay, I just move to a different location. The main thing for me in journaling is to start. I might not finish sorting things out in one setting, but I do see progress as my writing progresses. Some people like writing prompts to get them going. I've included some of these prompts in Chapter 3 – "Writing Prompts for You". In my daily "God Letter", I typically write after breakfast, occasionally drinking coffee. I do this at home mostly, but I've done this also at restaurants, too. Once I journal in the morning, I usually don't journal any more during the day. Things pile up each day. Some things are washed away during my sleep and dreams, but the lingering ones I write about. Each day is a new beginning with different topics to write about. I just write and write and write, filling up the page. I learned that if I stop and think about what I'm going to write, then I don't write anything or only what I "should" write about, avoiding the topics I "shouldn't" write about. This "filtering" does me no good at all, sanitizing my writing. I just blurt it out on paper, frequently between what looks like gibberish. My writing is only for me in most cases, these days. In this book, I gave you My Story, but this is highly atypical for me. I'm a very private introvert. I like to keep to myself, mostly. As I say, nowadays, I write only for myself and don't share it with anyone. In years past, I did share my writings with therapists and my support people – all to get better and stay better. For now, I don't feel like I need more therapy. I'm content with my support circle of friends and family. Yet, things change. I want to be open to getting a "tune-up" if needed. With all my journaling, I can give a therapist, a doctor, or other caring person a summary of "what's going on", rather than just rambling on and not getting to the point. We can get right into possible solutions rather than just diddling with the problem or problems. Sometimes, though, I just need to stop and go through the feelings, like grieving. All the words in the world won't make me feel better when I sense a great loss. This is not the time for journaling – it is a time for crying. In between the tears, I can write or call someone to try to sort things out, though. I think I've told you all I can about how I journal – and I've given you an example in the next chapter "My Story". If you have questions, let me know. I don't know everything but I do know what works for me.

By the way, this book is for information only and is not medical advice or any other kind of advice. You do what you think is best – and if you think you need professional health services, please do so. Don't let it pile up as I did earlier in life. In addition, I should say that Journaling does not take the place of professional counseling or medical assistance. It helps, but sometimes you might need a trained person to get from where you are now to where you want to be.

One more thing – YOUR journaling is for YOU for YOUR use – YOUR creation. You might want to keep it to yourself, though. Use your own judgment on who you want to share your thoughts and feelings with. I've found sometimes I share too much and later regret it.

My Story

THIS CHAPTER MIGHT be quite mixed-up and choppy, since I'm trying to write "off the top of my mind" over many days, telling my story. My handwritten usual journaling looks nothing like what you see in this book – it is messy and disorganized to others – yet it works for me. This chapter is minimally edited so as to show the "real me", instead of mincing my words, though, just to make it look good. I hope I don't offend anyone by telling how it was for me these last few years – but it was healing for me to write this and by sharing my story I hope to show others how journaling can be helpful to navigate the ups and downs of life. Here goes....

...I don't know when my angst started over the events of the last few years. All I know is that I was upset about the Pandemic and Politics mostly. Now I'm more concerned with the Economy, Inflation, prices going up, etc. I don't like it. It bothers me. Looking back, I think it started around the 2016 Presidential Election. I got all upset about one of the Presidential Candidates that he shouldn't act as he did. Generally, I was doing pretty well in life up until then. Before the Election, I was glued to the news, debates, and comments from others mostly related to the Candidate I didn't like. It became an obsession. It just didn't fit with my prior view of what a President should be and how one should act. During the Pandemic, I would have liked to have had a president that was a calming force, much like President F.D. Roosevelt and his Fireside Chats. Alas, that didn't happen. Later, I found out that there are very few requirements to be a President, according to the U.S. Constitution. Wow, did I learn something there! Currently, I think an unwritten requirement to be President is that they need lots and lots of money to pull it off – or even to be in the running. All this just irritated me. The 2016 Election did not fit the way I wanted it to, based on what I thought was right. Again, boy, did I learn something there. Things don't go my way, even if I want them to. I still wonder, "How could all this happen?"

Expanding on the above, I think what bothers me the most is that I'm afraid of someone becoming a dictator of the U.S., similar to what happened to other countries throughout history. It bothered me a lot when a president could seemingly say or do anything and get away with it, boldly I might add. It bothered me but yet much of the country supported this president, as shown by party support, money donated, religious promotion, followers – often violent and forceful, and almost half of the presidential votes. It seems scary even today that one person can have such a powerful effect on a party and some people, even if that person is out of office now. It bothered me that Electoral College votes could outweigh popular votes and more specifically state electors were not obligated to vote according to the state's popular votes – and scarier is that electors could be influenced by power and/or money. Wow! From what I saw, it seems like the government could be overtaken by violence, too. I don't know what could stop it if it ever starts. I'm afraid for my own and my family's safety. The country just doesn't seem safe today to me and maybe to others, too. It seems like the U.S. is evolving to "might makes right", money and power rules – no matter what, and being an isolated island in a world of countries, not caring what goes on anywhere else, except if it involves money or power. A lot of my angst, I think, springs out of how it was when I was a child. At that time, there was a lot of racial tension and the unsaid phrase was "White you're alright, brown stick around, black stay back". Yuck! I didn't like that then and I don't like it now. I still think that women are treated less than – I thought we were getting better but the last few years have proved me wrong. The same goes for those who are "marginal" – those considered as "outsiders", disabled, gender preference, marriage by same-sex people, etc. To me, it seems like we're going backward to a time when it was scary to live in the U.S. – the "Jim Crow" era, white supremacy, "us vs. them", etc. I was born in 1947 and talk of World War 2 was still on people's minds. The Holocaust had just ended. There was still hatred going on among many. Today, I still think of Air Raid Sirens instead of Weather Alerts. In 1947, the U.S. Civil War was still discussed – in fact, I once found a civil war cannon ball, or so I think it was. In addition, today there is talk of Civil War, too, and it is 2022. OK, I got it out. Enough of that. Time to get back to now. _Advice to Self_ – _Stop with the doomsday scenarios! Just stop it! It does you no good to sit and fret about what might happen. Just vote, encourage others to vote, and be done with it. Whatever happens after that is not up to you. You don't need to hear or see the blow-by-blow details (news) – it's not good for you. The sky is probably not going to fall. Trust, as best as you can, that things are going to work out. Tom, you've got a habit of worrying about many things that never happen – try to stop it - think about something else. Tom, you did good to get out your worst fears, now move on. If something disastrous comes up, deal with it then. In the meantime, You have a good, happy, healthy, successful life. Let others be. Move on Tom._

It also bothers and frightens me that Religions seem to be getting more powerful and influential over the last few years. I've been around long enough to remember experiencing or reading about how Religion has hurt people, e.g. The Crusades, the Inquisition, violence in the name of religion, forced religious conversion of Native American Children, abuse, racism, discrimination, proselytizing, some of my own religious upbringing (bullying/shaming/guilting/fearful), etc. I don't like it, but it seems like we're going backward to a time when religion did in fact have a great effect on politics, the governing/treatment of people, etc. _Advice to Self_ – _Stay out of it, Tom. Religions and religious people are going to do what they're going to do (or not do), whether or not you like it. That's just how it is. Learn from religions and religious people, if you can, otherwise just leave them alone. Be glad that you have a good personal relationship with_

God and leave it at that. Don't waste time and energy seeing what others are doing if it's not helpful to you. Stay tuned to your own God, Tom.

I have always been a worrier, in a state of continuous anxiety over one thing or the other. This probably relates to my early life, but that doesn't matter now. I'm an adult now – and wanting to be more relaxed about whatever goes on around me. Keep it calm inside. In fact, I found the book "Little Ways to Keep Calm and Carry On" by Mark Reinecke very helpful over the last few years with all the turmoil going on in the world and around me. I found out that "Keep Calm and Carry On" was on a British poster around World War II to improve morale. I like this since I felt like I and others were under a "Blitz" of evolving troubling events. I wanted a way out of my internal turmoil over what was going on in the world and I found comfort in this book.

I, like everyone, heard about Covid in late 2019, well into the 2016 Presidential Term. In the spring of 2020, the World Health Organization declared Covid a Pandemic. Yes, this was troubling to hear, but at that particular time, it didn't affect us personally, until the CDC guidelines were created. That was a big deal. Many places were closed and it was weird. Some parts of the world were in quarantine. We didn't have that where we live, but WOW, what a scary time. At that time, I, and I'm sure most of the world was glued to the news, picking up pieces of information from all over. Everyone had an opinion of what to do or not do. I was in severe turmoil with the governmental handling of this Pandemic and not knowing what to do or not do. I was so upset. That's all anyone was talking about – the Pandemic and Political Activities. I just didn't know whom to believe. Everyone from top-down to down-top had a plan of how to deal with Covid. Yikes, what to do next? I feel sad writing this even now since I felt so helpless in this situation. I just didn't know how to handle it. I and others searched for solutions and found few if any. I don't know if you remember at that time, but there was lots of innovation going on – some good, some not so good. The good that was happening was the public around the world were uniting to cope with the Pandemic. Some designed and made masks, since there was a shortage. The Internet was alive with people working together all around the world, sharing designs and DIY information. This was helpful to me and maybe to others to have "something to do" in the time of mix-up. Grocery stores were open at this time, but the shelves were becoming empty, due to hoarding, I guess. We still have a few things in our stockpile in the basement from those days. Yes, we followed CDC guidelines and local guidelines during the Pandemic, but some did not. At the time, this irritated me to no end, since I think all of us were so scared of getting Covid from others. To this day, we have not had Covid, but I think it is only a matter of time. I'm so glad we have the vaccination and I do thank President Trump for kick-starting Vaccine Production. That was good in my mind. Anyhow, getting back to what to do about Covid, I finally decided the best source of information was our own personal doctor. This made sense to me, since our doctor has advised us through many health challenges over the years. Yet, I was still glued to the news, politics, events, and social media until just recently – in fact, just in the writing of this book. Writing this book now is healing for me. I'm processing emotionally what happened in the past, and deciding how I want to act (not react) in the future. I went off the deep end over politics and the pandemic in the past – I was no longer thinking rationally and clearly, but instead a fusspot of emotions. I no longer want to live that way.

There were many shortages because of the pandemic and even today in 2022, there are shortages. We had to scrounge around looking for cat food – and even today some shelves are empty. I just found out that oil-based paint is not being stocked so much anymore. The paint store said that during the pandemic, management eliminated the slow-sellers. I think this happened in many places and in many ways. Companies had the time to re-evaluate how they want to go in the future, as well as individuals. Today, a big shortage is computer "chips" and actually, shortages of people to work in many businesses. There are many "now hiring" signs all over. I think people realized they didn't want to work so much, so long, and for so little – that they found new jobs and/or got more training for a better job. During the Pandemic, there were lots of "cleaners" – people in clinics, restaurants that were open, etc. that just cleaned tables, chairs, etc. Yes, there was and is government help along the way for people, industries, companies, etc. but that money is "drying up" – getting people, companies, industries, stock markets, etc. to "stand on their own" more.

The pandemic has moved on in 2022. Not many talk of it these days, except maybe as related to shortages, vaccine boosters, etc. I think, however, that many people were "left behind" – those who are "Covid Long-haulers", those who are now left with mental/physical illness as a result of Covid, and those who lost people or finances so much that they are paralyzed in life, stuck. I hope those people find relief. Maybe this book will give them hope to pick up the pieces as best as they can and move on – to maybe a new normal – but better than being stuck.

Another bug-a-boo for me has always been overthinking and seeking perfect solutions to things. You can just imagine how I was in a tiz, trying to figure out all that was happening over these last years and what was **I** going to do about it. Yuck. I wore myself out trying to figure out this mess going on around me. No one else seemed to have answers – at least <u>good</u> answers. There were and still are lots of opinions of what to do or not do going around. Listening to the news, government leaders, medical experts, politicians, and just about everyone else just overloaded me with information – and not a good solution amongst the lot! *<u>Advice to Self</u> – When faced with information overload and/or indecision – step back, think, relax, get information/advice from <u>trusted</u> information sources – then decide whether to act, wait, or not act at this time. Keep apprised of the situation from trusted advisors, though, in case further action is necessary.*

Wow, the Pandemic Guidelines meant that I could no longer see my family and friends in person, without risking one of us getting sick. I still grieve over not seeing our children and grandchildren very much at that time – lost opportunities. Most everything was closed except for "essential services" and "essential workers". During that time, I tried to thank the essential workers when getting gasoline or getting groceries, since I knew they were risking the health of themselves and their families by working – yet they had to pay the bills. Too bad. Again, I was perturbed at those not following CDC guidelines when around those workers. I just didn't like that, but I kept my masked mouth shut.

It was weird and inconvenient when we had to drop our car off for service. All I could do is to sanitize going in with a dispenser at the door, interact at a distance and masked, then go away until the car was fixed. Waiting rooms were closed. Public restrooms were closed. Many businesses were closed. Sometimes I just went for a walk or bike ride while waiting to get the car back – sometimes in the cold, snow, heat, rain, etc. I'm glad things are back to "normal" now.

Something unusual happened during the pandemic that I didn't plan on or even expect. As I said before only "essential" services were open. It was spring of 2020, I think, and I had just cleaned out the garden beds and was ready to take the bags to the local brush-recycling place. It was closed! Non-essential. So what do I do with all 20 or so bags of garden debris, much of it was still moist? It started to ferment in the bags and the bags were getting warm, as I had them in the garage. I started to worry about spontaneous combustion. Hmmm, what do I do now? I emailed the town/village we live in and told them of my predicament. Some people were still working in offices, or maybe at home, during that time. It took a while for a reply, but the answer was no – not then. Maybe others had the same problem as me, since the dumpsite did open sometime later. Good – it took me a while but I relieved myself of all this stinky stuff. Everything was weird at that time, people kept their distance, talked little, just did their business, and left. I think there is some carry-over of this today, that people just got used to being alone and apart. Maybe I'm wrong, but the world where I live seems to be quieter and less interactive than it used to be.

Maybe it was my imagination, but it seems like there were more construction projects going on during and after the Pandemic. This reminded me of all the construction projects that were funded by then-President Obama during the Great Recession of 2008-2009. At that time, there were major road/highway construction projects that went on. It was nice to see the multitudes of workers employed to rebuild the highways near us. I could see government-funded construction projects as a result of the pandemic, but it baffled me, and still baffles me, that there is so much private or commercial construction going on in such economic times as we have had and still have. Maybe I "missed the memo", as they say. Maybe more went on during the pandemic that I, or we, the public do not know about.

During the Pandemic, a good friend of mine died. She was 103 I think I remember. We talked, when she was alive, how this was the second pandemic she went through in her lifetime, although she was very young when the 1918 pandemic hit. Her family was not greatly affected by the first one because they lived in a rural area. We also discussed politics in her lifetime, what had changed, etc. As far as the economy, she had lived through the Great Depression, two world wars, and various other events in her lifetime. As I think of it now, it reminds me that things change, whether I like it or not. My friend always adapted to the changes in her life. Maybe that's why she lived such a long and good life. I didn't go to my friend's funeral because I don't like funerals, even if they're by video. My heart went out to those people who died during the pandemic with no family around, due to Covid restrictions. It bothered me on the news seeing so many dead and dying. It also bothered me seeing that people were not allowed near those dying or dead due to Covid. It makes sense, but it still must have been hard on the person dying and those close to them, as well as not being able to follow the traditions of the area. *Advice to Self* – *If you don't like what's happening around you, try to change it, and if that doesn't work, adapt and be happy with what you've got. Remember that all things change. Here in Wisconsin,*

I've heard that if I don't like the weather today, wait a day or so, and it will change. Life is like that, Tom.

I was so lonely at that time. I felt like an out-cast getting things curbside and having to hand sanitize anytime I touch something. I spent a lot of time outdoors during that time, since walking and bicycling were my only safe health options. The health clubs I went to were closed. You know some years before, I had a premonition that my enjoyment of health clubs would stop – and it did! So, I walked and walked and walked – each day no matter what the weather. I got so bored walking the usual paths that I started to explore and got on private property. As a result of my wandering, I got a ticket for walking on a railroad track. I sure didn't like that - $285, I think the fine was. As I look back, it was good, since I've had some close calls with trains in the past. Learning lesson, albeit expensive.

For many years, I was going to in-person support groups for my psychological and emotional health. No more during the Pandemic, and even today very few face-to-face meetings are going on, at least where I live. I'm so glad we have phone meetings, which I still regularly attend. These meetings help keep me more balanced in life and help me work out things. "ZOOM™" support meetings are available too, but I never tried them. I'm content with the phone meetings.

It's 2022 now and most things are wide-open to the public, if they can find workers, and if they didn't go out of business due to Covid Closures, e.g. restaurants, movies, etc. Locally, one of my support groups is thinking of re-starting with what we call "face-to-face" meetings. One meeting for sure I plan to go too, but maybe not others. I don't know yet. I'm somewhat fearful of going back, I'm not sure why. I've been quite content with phone meetings over these last few years. Yet, I still miss the personal contact of the meetings I used to go to before the Pandemic. Maybe I'm fearful because I'm a big-time introvert and the phone meetings were very safe, since no one knew whether I was there or not. I frequently just listened to meetings and found help in just doing that. *Advice to Self* – *Try, at least, Tom. Think about it. What do you have to lose? Take healthy risks in your "new normal" life. See how it goes. You can always go back...or not. At least give things a try. At least, keep an open mind and consider things as they come up.*

I think I was partially depressed during the last few years, but writing this book has helped me tremendously getting out from all the muck and mire of my negative thinking/feeling. I'm so glad I did as well as I did, though. Now is the time to heal from the past few years and move on – brighter.

At the time of this writing (mid-2022), the fear of Covid has diminished. Just about everything is open. Few people follow CDC guidelines, which I don't even check anymore. We still wear masks, social distance, and sanitize in some situations – but that is our choice. We want to stay healthy. As a sidelight, I recently talked to someone who worked at a food processing company and he told me they had to wear masks for 707 days! Wow, that must have been so hard – yet he endured and we all endured in our own ways.

The Pandemic stopped me in my tracks, like most people, forcing me to have time to think...feel...and decide what to do next. This is not the first time in my life, I've had a "wake-up call". About 40 years ago, I had a brain tumor and was off work for 6 months. I decided I needed some personal improvements – and I had plans to do so in the future. Well, I went back to work with all good intentions, then I fell back into my old ways again. Sometime later, I had supper with a fellow engineer whom I greatly admired. This person talked about getting some therapy to help his life. I was uncomfortable listening, since engineers just don't talk about personal stuff, and worse yet getting help for it. He went his way and I went mine. Sometime later, his words took root in my mind and I got some help too. As a result of help from others, I took myself apart and put myself back together again being the person I want to be – now and in the future. In doing so, I discarded all the useless beliefs and expectations that others wanted of me – and kept what was useful for me as an adult. Time passes - It's been good for many years – until the Pandemic-Politics mess came along. In writing this book, I'm taking myself apart and putting myself together again, since I realized I still needed more "improvements" so as to act/respond to life better than reacting to life and its events. I'm still working on it, but this book is helping me sort things out. This time around, in retrospect, I just did not manage the stressors very well at all – and it got the best of me. I know better – I've taken courses in Stress Management and even write about how to manage Stressors for long-term relief from stress. Alas, I didn't follow my own advice and I got sucked into what was going on around me. I definitely was in the reaction mode, stressing out, for many months, if not years. I'm getting better now. I don't know if this book is helping you, but it is certainly helping me. Good luck in sorting yourself out, if you want.

I'm sure everyone had more than the Pandemic/Politics going on in their lives too. For us, one of the long-term stressful/sad events was taking care of our very old, sickly, cat. Yes, eventually, the kitty died, but for a long time we took care of her and it was hard. During the Pandemic, we had to sit out in our car in the cold and heat, while she was being treated, since no one could go inside. They came out and got 99, our kitty, and brought her out when done. Sad, hard, but necessary. We take good care of our pets right up to the end. On a happier note, we have a new kitty now, and can now go into the vet's office waiting room.

Speaking of not being able to go in, did I tell you about my annual health checkup with my doctor during the Pandemic? Well, it was due and I wanted to be checked to maintain my good health – but I didn't want to go in, even if masked and socially distanced, as was done at that time. So what am I going to do? I just didn't want to be unnecessarily exposed to "sickies". I was scared for my own health and didn't want to bring "Covid Cooties" home. I've got a wonderful doctor and he agreed to meet me outside at the picnic table. He had his laptop and we talked. I think I still had to go inside for blood tests, but that was just a quick in/

out and sometimes I actually held my breath around others who looked sick. I just didn't want to get sick. That is one of the good memories of the Pandemic and how we, and everyone, innovated solutions.

I think I told you a little bit about grocery shopping. Yes, stores were open and at that time everyone had to wear masks and social distance – or leave the store. It was kind of scary as it reminded me of when I lived through the Detroit Riots in 1967. Others and I obeyed the curfew and other "guidelines" because we were so fearful, due to the military presence on the streets. The Pandemic was certainly not that bad, but for me, it brought back memories. Maybe it was like that for you too. Anyhow, from what I remember, customers could only have one cart and had to follow CDC guidelines. We did, and some didn't. I got my nose out of joint, but that's nothing new. We grocery shopped and the checkout lines were throttled by an employee only allowing one checkout at each checkout station. Each person in the long waiting line was distanced 6 feet away from each other. They had lines on the floor. The waiting line extended way back into the store. At checkout, they had Plexiglas shields and copious applications of cleaning solutions before and after each customer. There was no drive-up, so we had to manually load our own car, even in the winter snow and cold. We, as well as others, survived and have lived to tell about it. ☺ During the Pandemic, many chose to make online orders and have them delivered or loaded by a store employee into the car's trunk/back without any contact with the customer. Curbside service was all that was available at many stores, libraries, and just about anywhere. From what I remember, pharmacies were still open to the public to pick up prescriptions. Many chose drive-through, as we did. I see many pharmacies, food places, etc. are now offering more home delivery since the pandemic too. Times have changed and I have changed too, as many have, I bet.

The other day was a "Pandemic Day" for me. It is 2022 and the Pandemic is virtually over, but there are things that I still want to keep doing that I did or didn't do with the Pandemic going on. One of those things that I missed over the last year or so was just walking or biking, listening to podcasts, or talking with friends on the phone, while out and about. During the Pandemic, I would just get out of the house every day, no matter what, for exercise and my own mental health. I dressed up appropriately depending on the weather, got my podcasts going, and got my feet going. I learned so much over those months and years, I can't even begin to tell you. Some of my favorite podcasts or "PLAYAWAY™" books were "A Brief History of Everyone Who Ever Lived: The Human Story Retold Through Our Genes" by Adam Rutherford tracing all the way back to Neanderthals and also several by Stephen Covey on the "7/8 Habits of Highly Effective People". I also listened to short stories and episodes of the Moth Radio Hour. Sometimes I even cried at what I heard, whether the tears were for current events in my own or past life – or hearing about someone else's story. In between, I may have swatted at mosquitoes or black flies, but I kept on going. Sometimes I'd see people on the trails, but at that time, we kept our distance. I didn't wear a mask when outdoors, but some people did. It seemed like we respected each other, chatted a little bit at a distance, and went our own way. Yes, I miss that, and will continue to have "Pandemic Days" where I bring back activities that were useful or helpful to me at that time.

Another good thing from the Pandemic was starting to call our oldest son once a week or so. Up until then, I only called once in a while. It's really nice keeping up with him, his life, and his family. Good feeling. A good memory from the Pandemic was seeing fathers play with their children in their yards – this brought a tear to my eye, since many fathers, like me, just didn't have the time to do that when working full-time. It's 2022 now and I don't see that as much now. Too bad, in one sense. Another good thing was seeing how people "coped around" events and activities, e.g. putting wrapped treats into little bags for the "trick or treaters" in 2020. We had a card table in the garage, keeping social distance, and supplying hand wash, too. You'd be surprised how people innovated and "designed around" obstacles and still stayed safe. I think I remember a group of biomedical engineering students in Uganda designing a ventilator with just bits and pieces of available material. This is an example of how people coped in the "Other 90% of the World" who just don't have the money, resources, etc. that the developed countries have. I tear up just thinking of this and remembering pictures of those in poverty countries at that time – sometimes still smiling – sometimes crying – just trying to live, stay safe and healthy, take care of their families and other responsibilities, and eke out a meager living. Bless them, I say. Those are the real heroes, too.

It was quieter during the Pandemic with more people staying at home. There was less traffic. It seemed to me that people were somewhat calmer and got along better despite what we all had to do or not do to avoid Covid. Maybe we all had a common purpose then and our differences somehow melted.

It's 2022 now and I hear political rumblings starting again. I'm so glad I almost entirely divorced myself from the political news and those talking about politics. In my travels now, when I hear others talking about politics, I avoid them. No sense in stirring myself up unnecessarily. I feel so glad I voted in the latest election near me earlier this week. My job is to vote, and maybe encourage others to vote, but that's it. I can't do anything more, productively, as an average citizen. It does me no good to discuss/argue politics with others – all that happens is that I come away with a bad feeling, all worked up – and I don't want to do that anymore.

I was born in the U.S. and I am grateful for that, knowing that I'm better off than most of the world. Saying that, even if things don't go my way and there are some people I don't like, I still want to stay here and make my own life here. I can stay away from those who bother me for the most part. I can adapt to the ups and downs created by political decisions – I have to. I can also try to add to making the world a little better. If I move somewhere else, there's always trouble there too. There is no perfect place to live. I can have a good life here – and I intend to make the most of it here.

Our local libraries were helpful to me during the Pandemic. They were closed altogether at one time, I think, but then offered curbside service. This was nice for me, since I could still enrich my life with books, audiobooks, magazines, etc. In fact, one library offered a "Surprise Me" package of magazines, based on my interests. This widened my perspective, by reading other than my usual magazines. People were so friendly handing out library materials – at a distance though, on a separate table. Everywhere, and I mean everywhere, had hand sanitizers available. One library had a giant sign in their window saying that Wi-Fi was available outside the building. More than once, I saw someone on a picnic table or in the parking lot making use of the Wi-Fi, even if the library was closed. Sad, yet resourceful, too.

It's 2022 now and even the CDC has loosened up their guidelines due to various factors – the major threat has passed for now – but it sounds like Covid, and its nasty cousins, are here to stay, much like the common cold and/or influenza. Adapt and carry on, I guess. We still follow CDC guidelines and our personal doctor's additional personalized guidelines for our own health and for the sake of others around us – whether others do so or not. It's our decision. From what I see today, most healthcare facilities still require masks at least, though.

During the height of the Pandemic, we had to go to a Major Healthcare Facility in a large city. This place was one of the facilities that handled the very serious Covid cases, as well as everyday healthcare. We were there for another healthcare reason, though. Anyhow, they were very strict in their protocol and just didn't allow anything else. In that facility, rules were enforced to the max – and rightly so, we thought, since very sick people were on the wards. We completed our visit and went back home, but I still remember how strict they were. They needed to be. Glad to get back home.

It bothered me to see pictures and hear stories of those who were on the "front lines" of hospitals, clinics, nursing homes, etc. They looked so weary, dirty, and sick to me, even if they were healthy workers, who

I'm sure were checked daily for Covid. Some doctors and nurses even had to stay at the hospital and not go home to their families. It was a greater risk to the family to go home than to stay at the hospital. Most hospitals switched to only pre-packaged food in the cafeteria and disposable plates/eating utensils – and much of this still goes on today from when I last visited a local hospital. When in the hospital during the peak, many of the workers were dressed in full protective suits, masks, gloves, and face shields. Some even had respirators, like scuba divers use, to breathe other than contaminated air.

What was even worse was to see the "other 90%" of the world who didn't have the money or fancy stuff we have in the developed countries. They had to make do with what they had and just had to mingle to stay alive. Some examples are highly populated communities where it just was not possible to adequately social distance – no room to do so. Many poorer countries just don't have the doctors, hospitals, and medicines that we in developed countries, like the U.S., have. We are so lucky. It was sad to see in the poorer countries how the dead had to be treated to prevent further contamination – mass burials, cremations, etc. People just couldn't touch the people who died from Covid or get sick themselves. Covid turned the world upside down. Some made it, others didn't, but I think all of us were affected by Covid in some way or another. The physical threat of Covid seems to be resolved for most people, worldwide, here in 2022, but I still think the mental/emotional scarring will continue. That's one of the reasons I'm writing this book – to help myself and maybe you as a reader. It helps me to write these memories, process them internally, and move on to my "new normal". Later in this book are questions (writing prompts) to jog your memory if you want.

Somewhere I heard that a Writer writes what they think and a Painter paints what they feel. I guess I'm writing as a Writer and Painter at the same time, since I'm not only reciting events but also adding how these events affected me emotionally and personally. I hope you find it as helpful as I am.

I heard the other day that the powers at be are just giving up, more or less, with guidelines, realizing that people are going to do what they do...or not do...no matter what Healthcare Professionals advise. That's a big lesson I've learned, too. Moreover, in my case, I try to just ignore what others do or don't do and not get upset.

Related to the paragraph above, the World Health Organization, the CDC here in the U.S., and other Public Health Organizations did provide guidelines for what to do and not do during the Pandemic. Much of this was about masking, social distancing, and sanitation. In addition, sometimes quarantines and/or lockdowns were advised. Here in Wisconsin, where I live, the Governor did make Mandates, but they were impractical to enforce by local officials, so the police/sheriff said. Ultimately, these mandates were overruled by the Wisconsin Legislative Branch and maybe even the Judicial Branch. So here in Wisconsin, at least, everyone did what they wanted to do or not do. This was troubling for me. It seemed like there was a divide between what was best for the health of people and what was good for business/jobs (money). This still troubles me but I'm learning just to "get over it". In my mind, the health of people is more important than money, at least for me. But, again, it doesn't matter, since now and in the Pandemic, people are going to do as they wish - guidelines/mandates or not. This should not be surprising to me, since some people ignore mandates when evacuation is advised/mandated in hurricane zones, here in the U.S. Again, I'm trying to not get all worked up about what others do or don't do   and just do what is best for us.

As I said earlier, I'm so glad that then-President Trump pushed along Vaccine Development (Operation Warp Speed). Yes, this was great, and I really appreciate a way out of the Pandemic/Covid. What I didn't like was that the technology was not made Public Domain for all to use around the World. I think this should have been done since the vaccine development was done with U.S. Tax Dollars and the rest of the World was suffering (For humanitarian reasons). This did not happen, for the most part. It just seemed wrong to me that people should profit when we paid them to do it. Alas, I got my nose out of joint, <u>again</u>. Ouch.

On the brighter side, I learned a lot during the Pandemic via Online Classes, learning how to write and publish books. This kept my mind busy, and off all my various Pandemic/Politics gripes. I had started writing just before the Pandemic, since I couldn't find work that I liked anywhere else. It seemed like a good thing to do. I liked the idea of making some money, helping people, and leaving a legacy. I'm not making much money, but I think it is good for me to do. Anyhow, I published my first book in March of 2020 and now have eight or so books published. My writing gives me purpose in life and keeps me busy. I wrote several books during the Pandemic, mostly around the psychological/emotional side of Covid. Maybe I'll re-write some of these someday to better reflect Post-Pandemic conditions.

As long as I'm leaving a legacy, I thought I'd tell you about what I was posting on social media during the height of the Pandemic. I think Pandemic teams should have Behavioral Scientists included too, as well as Mental Health Specialists. I even wrote to President Biden to add these folks to his Covid Task Force. Maybe future Epidemic/ Pandemic Task Force Teams will consider this. From what I see, people just don't want to consider the psychological/emotional side of health/ sickness – both patients and doctors. Yet it is there. I hear it now how the Pandemic has created PTSD for frontline workers – how children have more mental health problems now due to the Pandemic – plus the ongoing stress of what's going on next with Covid Cousins, Politics, Economics, and who knows what else.

As I said earlier, I kept my sanity and peace by listening to audiobooks as I walked or bicycled day after day. Even today, I can remember where I was when I heard a particular segment of an audio program. How interesting life became during those moments – hearing about the kind of ink used on the walls of early cave dwellers – and how successful people live – and listening to story episodes of a boy who wanted to be a writer and how he attracted the attention of accomplished writers. It was almost like I was in a different world at that time listening to what excited my soul.

Something else that bothered me during the Pandemic was how Politicians and Churches had opinions on how Covid should be treated. This just did not seem right to me that they should get involved – and yet many followed the Church's and Politician's Guidelines over the CDC Guidelines and probably their own doctor's advice. During the Pandemic and even now, I don't think I heard a doctor go against CDC Guidelines and Vaccinations – but I'm sure there might be some. Anyhow, as I said earlier, we finally decided to try to ignore all the jibber-jabber and do what our personal doctor advised us to do and not do. Earlier I would hear some people talking about not "getting the jab" because their church leader told them so. That's okay I guess for them, but not good for me. I've heard how vaccination and politics are even splitting families and friends apart. Wow, such power. I get nervous around situations where people are so locked into their thinking. But then, I do that too sometimes I guess. I try not to though.

The January 6 White House Attack bothered me and scared me. How can they have so much power and get away with so much, I thought to myself? Even today, it drags on and for me, it is scary to think about what is next, with future elections. Yuck. As I said earlier, I lived through the 60's Detroit Riots where Military Tanks ruled the streets. Such a scary time for me. There must have been lots of racial tensions leading up to the riot, but I was too young and away from it to notice. I do remember black/white tension though, that's for sure. It was there when I was growing up with white-only drinking fountains and toilets, as an example. I am white but I still felt sorry for how the blacks were treated. Frequently they were ignored, at best, and beaten up/killed at the worst. I remember those days. I remember the Ku Klux Klan, too. I went to a Trade School instead of the Local High School and my best friend there was black. We both had an interest in Electronics. One time we went to an electronic parts store and the clerk would only talk to me and not my friend. How uncomfortable that was for me and how it must have made my friend feel. It went both sides – whites didn't want me to associate with blacks – and other black students didn't want me to associate with my black friend. Once I got cornered by a bus stop in Detroit by a crowd of black students who were roughing me up, one even had a knife, but fortunately, the police came by and broke it up. I'm telling these stories, since that's how I'm feeling today with all this Political, Racial, and Religious Tension going around. There's even talk of a Civil War! I just don't like it. I've seen bad things happen and I don't want them to happen again. Too much tension. I guess for now, wait and see, and try to relax myself. Riots, Tensions, Etc. – there's not much I can do about it except to keep myself out of the turmoil – to not be part of the problem but be my own solution. _Advice to self_ - stay out of trouble.

I've been churning around in my mind what bothers me most about Politics – and I think it is how money and powerful people have such a great effect on the Government and Legal System, e.g. lobbying, gerrymandering, enormous campaign/personal contributions, violence/bullying, etc. Another thing that bothers me is that the World of Politics is so much different than the rest of the working world. In my experience, most jobs have clearly defined job descriptions and requirements – politics doesn't seem to have that. Also, most jobs have frequent performance reviews and consequences if goals are not met – politics does not seem to have that. Usually, "false advertising", making claims that don't happen, outright lying, is just wrong on so many levels – yet it is acceptable to politicians, and even the public! In addition, most jobs are filled through a logical employment process – politics does not seem to have that, instead relying on the emotion of the voters, and the influence of money/power to get into office. Sometimes, I think that what we see, as a public, is an illusion of what others want us to see. Bad thinking. Politics did not bother me as much when I was younger – I think I've got too much time on my hands as an older person. *Advice to Self – Now and in the Future – Tom, MYOB, stop thinking about politics so much, and just do your best at voting and encourage others to vote – then let it go and get on with your life – forget about the political outcomes. If something comes up, deal with it and move on. Get over it, Tom, and don't let Politics get you down!*

When I was younger, I didn't pay much attention to politics and the news in general. I voted sometimes in the Presidential Elections when a candidate really appealed to me – or to keep the other candidate out, whom I didn't like. I didn't research candidates like I do now and try to vote intelligently. I just voted on who looked good and sounded good – which I think most people do now, anyhow. At that time in my life, I was so busy working very demanding jobs, trying to be a good father, husband, son, provider, etc. Furthermore, I was indeed "hiding from life" with overeating, excessive alcohol, over-working, and other compulsions. Too bad, but that's the way it was. It wasn't until I had my "brain tumor wake-up call" that I described earlier in this chapter that I got some help. So what am I saying? I think politics bothers me more today because my life is far less active, being "retired", so I've got much more time to think, ruminate, get in a bad mood, etc. Well, as I said in this chapter, I don't want to do that anymore. I got sucked into monitoring the news (all bad, of course, like the news is) incessantly. I just couldn't get enough of it. I was like a moth drawn to a flame, as they say. It bothered me that the same news was repeated, day after day, with different wording or spin on it, and seemingly nothing ever got resolved. It also bothered me when something was in the news, then not ever finished or resolved – it's like it never happened. Well, I'm out of it now and plan to stay out of it. *Advice to Self – Find a life, Tom. You just can't handle listening/seeing the news – so stay away from it. It's not good for you. It's like poison to your soul, Tom. If something is really important, you'll hear about it in some way, but don't go seeking bad news.*

Something that helped me during the Pandemic was an old netbook that I had set up to continuously show webcams around the world, using EarthCamTV™. Seeing others living their lives helped me get out of myself and my little closed-in world at the height of the Pandemic. Yes, I saw fewer people in Times Square and at the beaches in Florida, and mentally counted, sometimes, how many were wearing masks and how many were not – fuming away, sometimes depending on my mood. In general, though, I found these webcam views comforting and it got my mind off how lonely I was. Yet, there was sadness, too, seeing the lack of people out and about – Ferris wheels stopped and dark – New York Times Square vacant – and much more – yet it got better as time went on with vaccinations and easing of guidelines. I even sent a thank-you card to EarthCamTV™ saying how much they helped me during the Pandemic. Surprisingly, they got my note and sent me a cap. I like the cap and still "armchair watch" the world even today. The webcams I like most are the most unique ones, I think, like the elephant watering holes somewhere in Africa or maybe the Philippines. Here in 2022, there are some books from writers around the world describing what it was like to live, or at least, try to live, as best as they could with Covid running rampant, even more so than here in the U.S. One book of these stories is "And we came outside and saw the stars again : writers from around the world on the COVID-19 pandemic" by Ilan Stavans (Editor).

For many months during the height of the pandemic, all non-essential businesses were closed, which included barbers and hair stylists. Well, my hair didn't stop growing, so I got a cheap electric hair trimmer to cut my own hair in the garage. It worked pretty good, albeit a little uneven when I first started. I got better as time went on. I still do this today, cutting my own hair, to help manage our budget in these times of economic inflation. I have liked finding cheaper ways ever since I was a child. My parents lived through the Great Depression of the 30's and it was reflected in their words and actions. We didn't have a lot of money – I guess you'd call us lower middle-class today – One time I remember my mother was worried that all they had left was $4.00 until my Dad got paid. My mother didn't work and about the only job my dad could do was "plant protection" (guard) at Chrysler's in Detroit, due to him having Parkinson's. It's a wonder he could do any job at all in the health condition he was in. He tried though. The greatest lesson I learned from my dad was to get up again. He fell so many times in his life, due to Parkinson's, but he always got up again. I feel sad writing this. I miss my dad. Anyhow, where was I going with this? – Oh, yeah, economy. When I was a kid, my mother had a book about 1,000 ways to save money. I liked reading that book, maybe because it had so many ideas on how to do things differently and cheaper. Another reason I "live within our means" is that we, as a couple, got into financial trouble many years ago with overspending, relying too much on credit cards, etc. – We went to Budget Counseling where they taught us how to manage our money better. We learned our lesson, mostly don't get too deep in debt for no good reason. At that time, they even advised freezing our credit card in a block of ice in the freezer – to give us time to think before we act. Today, we do better with our money management.

What a mess it is with the Economy – during and after the Pandemic. I just can't figure it out. It baffled me how people could keep on going despite being laid off from their jobs, due to Covid closures. At that time, I did hear how people struggled to make ends meet using their savings, unemployment payments, and sometimes Covid Relief Checks. Some were severely affected by Covid and others were less affected, e.g. farmers, essential workers, etc. It was interesting to me that the laid-off workers had time to think about what they wanted to do moving forward with their lives. Some went back to school, some were reluctant to go back to their old jobs for health or other reasons, and some found work-from-home jobs. The effect today, 2022, is that there are "Hiring Now" Signs all over. Some businesses have even closed due to not being able to find workers. It's a "workers' market" now and people seem to be more selective on the kind of work they want to do moving forward.

The minimum wage has increased, I think, due to Covid and the lack of people willing to work for minimum wage anymore. _Advice to Self_ – Be glad you have what you have. Stop trying so hard to make more money and/or get people to like your work. Maybe what you do in writing will never make much money, but it might help someone – be glad of that. You have a purpose, Tom, and that is very important in life. Keep doing what you're doing, Tom, unless situations change. Be happy, healthy, and content with what you have.

I listen to a local radio station sometimes and one of the hosts is a famous singer and songwriter. During the pandemic, he described the plight of musicians, other performers and creators of art in one form or another. He asked people to support musicians and others, since many concerts were canceled due to Covid. Some musicians used other means to sell their work – online concerts, etc. Radio and Television had to change too, due to Covid. There were no live audiences at that time. Programmers, Hosts, and others worked together online to produce programs. I've even heard of a "Covid Concert" via ZOOM™. Much much less casual and I loved it! Sometimes you could hear a dog barking in the background of a show being produced, since everyone was at home at the computer making the shows. Covid made work-from-home explode and many like it today. Some won't go back to their old jobs the way they were – most want hybrid (being on-site some and working from home some) – some want all work from home. Now, in 2022, we have choices – work onsite, hybrid, and work from home. Who would have ever thought this? Again, this is a "worker's market" and to keep good workers employers are forced into negotiating work conditions with the employees. Each employee has different priorities in life and employers are listening more now and trying to accommodate as much as they can. Wow, times have changed from years ago, and just before Covid. Amazing – and I think it is good. I dislike formality and doing things a particular way – just because it's the way we always did it. I ran into opposition when I was working many times trying to change old systems or ways of doing things. At that time, employers could "call the shots", but maybe people, in general, are more open-minded on how to "get the job done" – in whatever way makes sense.

During the Pandemic, I didn't mind watching or listening to real-life stories and even news about how people were coping and finding solutions. When listening to those programs or news, I mostly felt sad and fearful. Hearing how politics was involved just angered me. I listened to audio stories too as I walked and walked about how the Pandemic had changed their lives. One story I remember was how a particular teacher somewhere "let down her hair" and became more personal with her students – hearing the stories of their lives and sharing some of her life, too. The students thrived on that and they became closer. I also saw on the news how someone had hung up a clear plastic tarp so they could visit and even hug family members, with the tarp protecting them from personal contact. I also saw in the news about the front-line healthcare workers, all completely garbed up, and forced to do "meatball surgery/ healthcare" due to the number of sick people. Doctors, hospitals, and clinics were only open to those who were indeed sick. Elective surgery/ treatment was on hold for a long time. I thought it was very nice how my physical therapist would call her patients to see how they were, when she was out of work (due to the pandemic) – only the most serious were allowed in for treatment. Tough times for all – we coped and managed – and in 2022 the Pandemic is mostly over, for now, they say. Covid and its nasty relatives still pop up here and there – and Covid Long Haulers are still struggling – but life goes on. We made it this far. Some made it, some didn't.

As I was watching how hard it was for front-line doctors, nurses, and others to treat those with Covid who did not get vaccinated, it bothered me. I can only imagine how angry the caregivers were, knowing that the sick patients in front of them had chosen not to follow medical advice and were now sick – exposing the caregivers and their families to Covid. I shouldn't be surprised since many folks just don't follow *medical advice, in general, and that's how it is. <u>Advice to Self</u> – MYOB, Tom. Others are going to do what they're going to do or not do, whether you like it or not. Get over it. Do your best to stay healthy and let others manage their own health in the way they want to. Don't get upset over others' actions/inactions – it's not good for you – and certainly not good for them if you "advise" them on how to live their lives.*

I don't know what you're thinking as you read "My Story", if you are. Perhaps, you think of this as a gripe session or the ramblings of an older person with nothing better to do. I suppose it is. I like it since it is helping me sort out the past and make plans for the future. I like adding the "<u>*Advice to Self*</u>" ditties I add here and there – they're laying down stepping stones for me to continue on with my life, after being stuck in the mental muck that I was in over the last years, some with the Pandemic, but much more with Politics.

Moving on with my story, it frightens me to see how militaristic and how angry people are these days. Average everyday guns don't bother me, since they've been around forever. What frightens me are angry people with guns and especially assault weapons. It reminds me of the Detroit Riots which I described earlier. I don't know the answer and pretty much stay out of it – and especially stay away from angry people, in general. I did feel very sad when people were killed in recent local/world events, especially children. It bothered me and still does when police officials let their anger/discrimination get the best of them and use excessive force and/or shooting. It bothered me hearing of how George Floyd died. Again, I don't know the answers, and I'm sure most police officials are doing their best. Policing is a tough job. As long as we're on this topic, I do feel bad about the War in Ukraine and other troubling events throughout the world. I also feel bad about how wars affect citizens (collateral damage is the term, I guess). I also feel bad about how wars, in general, have adversely affected veterans with PTSD. It must be very hard. My heart goes out to them. Yes, I'm a softhearted person, probably way too sensitive, but that's how I am – get over it. I'm me and I like me.

I've learned that some people like me, some people don't like me, and the majority of people don't even know I exist.

So what can I do to maybe make this a better world? Maybe my story will help you or others. Maybe my example will encourage you to write or tell your story. I just blurt it out, as it is, not screening my words or thoughts too much. That's how I healed in the past – turning myself inside out – to see what is good to keep and what to discard. I want to get better and stay better. Maybe you do too. I wish you well.

During the Pandemic, a lot of people had to stay at home. Students had online learning for some time. This must have been hard on students, teachers, schools, and many more. What did evolve out of all this, however, was the rise of online learning and work-from-home opportunities that maybe weren't there before. Some good usually comes out of most situations. It's hard to change, though, as many remember. Change is hard for most people.

Working from home became the norm for many, as I just mentioned. This upset the work world, since employers wanted people to come back to work on-site and many workers just did not want to. Everything became casual and the usual stuffiness of many work interactions went by the wayside. This seems to be part of the new normal, which I entirely support. Much more is happening online today. I don't know if this is good or not – but it certainly is what it is, and probably will not ever go back to the way it was. As far as schooling, there was some concern that children were becoming withdrawn as a result of a lack of socialization. Here we are in 2022 and much has returned to "normal" but not completely. We, as a society, learned there are many more options to life than what we were doing before. Some liked this, others didn't.

I think many good things happened as a result of the Pandemic. One good thing is that my family and I are healthy, despite Covid around us. We, as a society, now have a proven vaccine for Covid. The Pandemic was a game –changer for many things. People started asking, "Why am I doing this?" and maybe finding a better job fit or deciding on further education. Work from home has skyrocketed, allowing people to work more casually and be with family more. Many innovations were created over the last few years, out of necessity. Virtual Medical Visits are now available much more. It seems like the healthcare system was streamlined during the pandemic, getting rid of the old ways of doing things, as needed. I think the drive for perfection was questioned and some people, like me, realized how good we have it.

By nature, I'm more of an Introvert, so social isolation did not affect me as much as others. I had a friend who was very much a people person. He thrived on social interaction and didn't know what to do with himself during the pandemic. He was not computer-savvy so did not have the option to virtually meet with others. He was elderly and in pretty good health when the pandemic began, but I could see a slow deterioration of his health, both physical and mental. Everything became so hard for him. He did have a phone and TV, though. He often talked about what he heard on the news. He was frightened and mad at what was going on in the world, as he related to me. He missed his wife and daughter who had previously died some time back. I did take him to some medical visits and later out to eat, now and then, but life was just not the same, as before the Pandemic. He died earlier this year and I miss him. I miss the way he was, not how he became. I don't know whether his physical conditions, of which he had many, some very serious, precipitated his death or his mental/emotional health. I think it was both. I think a person has to have good mental health/mood/ attitude to have good physical health and visa-versa.

As I think I said before, I published my first book just before Covid began. My mental health/attitude/mood shifted and became more adversely pronounced after we were in the pandemic for a while. I was so low walking through a cemetery that I stopped at a local religious retreat house. No one looked "at home", but then someone came out to get the mail. We chatted for a while, then I just started crying saying what was going on in my life. He listened, gave me a few words of inspiration, then

I moved on. I sent him a thank you card for that. That effort got me out of the "dumps" temporarily. I then wrote some further books on the psychological/emotional aspect of the pandemic, focusing on how stress affected the immune system. No one seemed very interested in hearing about this stuff, then, and even now. I guess my books kept me going and I was trying to help others. Most people don't want to hear about the "soft side" of anything. Everyone was focused on the physical aspects of Covid and not looking at the "big picture" of what else was going on. I posted on social media about mental health during the pandemic, but no one seemed very interested. I even wrote to the CDC and maybe the World Health Organization encouraging them to give tips/advice on how to cope mentally and emotionally. I was pleased when the CDC did include this later – maybe my efforts did help, who knows? Anyhow, today, most people just don't talk too much about the pandemic and how it affected them. I guess most people are just able to pick themselves up and get back to life. I guess I'm not that resilient. Maybe others are not that way, too, and that's why I'm writing this book – to remember the past, learn from it, and move on. In writing my story here, I am doing just that.

Wow, this writing is sure helping me sort things out. I can only do this journaling for a little while, before it tires me out, but the "sorting out" continues in my head and even in my dreams, sometimes. Amazing, isn't it?

I think what bothered me most was that a President did not act the way I think a President, or anyone else for that matter, "should" act. I guess I was basing my "should" on what I learned early in life, probably in kindergarten – play nice, don't bully, respect others, no name-calling, be honest – tell the truth, no violence, follow the "golden rule", try to get along with others, play fair, talk nice, be nice, be kind to others, share and share alike, etc. I was also basing my "should" on what I learned in school about Democracy and how the branches of government worked together to achieve the will of the people. I also learned, at an early age, that the laws are for everyone – equal justice for all. In school and at church I was taught that everyone was equal. Even as an adult, I like standardization – same for all. What happened a few years ago politically really upset me, since what was happening veered so far away from what I was taught and how I personally try to live. I'm afraid this will happen in the future and I will do my part by voting and encouraging others to vote. Beyond that, I can't do more, I just can't. Worrying about it doesn't help. Talking politics certainly does not help! I guess that's why they say "don't talk about politics or religion". Lesson learned. Hovering over the news does not help either – this just "fans the flames" of my worrisome nature. _Advice to Self_ – *Grow up. Times are different, now. You be the way you think people should act, instead of looking at others – what they're doing or not doing. Yes, vote and be done with it – much like "flushing the toilet" or "releasing a balloon"! You can't handle much more than that. Get on with your own life, Tom, and stop looking at others. Be the person you think you should be – follow your own "internal compass", morals, and goals in life. Let others be themselves and move on with your own life. If something comes up, deal with it. Much talk in politics never much happens. Don't go trying to predict future actions on a few shreds of political information. Stay in today and deal with today's problems as they come, Tom.*

Yes, you can probably see I'm one of those who find fault in just about everything and everyone. It's a habit and I'm working on changing it. Yes, I don't like lots of things that go on around me. So, what am I going to do about it? I could get all worked up or I can let the change begin with me. I do some of that already. Some time ago, I read an article on how precious water is to most of the world. It impressed me so much that I now do what I can to save water usage, e.g. take "military showers" instead of letting the shower go on and on for a long time using both water and energy to heat the water. Yes, I notice others using more water and energy, but it makes me feel good knowing that I'm doing my part. I'd like to do more actions like that – to change _my_ behaviors and attitudes to perhaps counter-balance the actions or inactions of others. _Advice to Self_ – _Yes, change you, Tom, and let others be._

When writing I like to stream "Outback Radio 2WEB" from Australia. I like the mental image this station and its location conjures up in my mind – where I'm out on my own writing in the "outback" of my life.

Some people that seem to reflect my own personality are President Abraham Lincoln, President Jimmy Carter, President Obama, Mr. Rogers, George Washington Carver, Grover from SESAME STREET™, Robin Williams, Nikola Tesla, and more that I can't think of now. Now, maybe you can see how I got so upset over the political actions over the last few years considering my personality and make-up.

In telling my story here, I should say that I do frequently imagine there is a problem, when in fact there is no problem. I live in between a world of imagination and reality. I imagine what might happen, especially if I do this or that action. Maybe this is a carry-over from my "caveman" ancestors where there was real danger most, if not all, the time. This is part of me and I'm working on it. My mind gathers pieces of information and tries to reach a conclusion and maybe a plan of action. I react to life. During these last years, I think I was overloaded with "what if's". I don't want to do "doomsday planning" like some are doing. I want to live in today and deal with today's challenges and enjoy today. There is no danger today in my life. Sometimes, to help me cope, I ask myself "Is it okay NOW, Tom" – the answer is always "Well, Yes". I also have found it beneficial to "just think about something else" – to shift my thinking to something I can do something about   especially something I want to do – in essence, keep my mind busy on productive or enjoyable activities. In the future, I want to respond, and maybe act, on life. Looking back over the last few years, I fretted a lot about what was happening around me. I got all upset and what was worse is that I couldn't do anything about it – or so I thought. Maybe that's why I got the book "Stay Calm and Carry On". I knew I was in trouble with my thinking and feeling. I had checked out that book before – and I used it this time, too, to sort out my thinking.

I realized during these last few years how biased, opinionated, and prejudiced I really am underneath it all. I say diversity is great, yet these last few years I just couldn't accept that people were not doing what I thought they should be doing. I learned a giant lesson that "people are going to do what they're going to do...or not do". I also realized that this is a big world with lots of diverse people of all kinds and in many ways. Some people I like, some people I don't like, and that's okay. In the past, I learned that some people like me, some people don't, and most of the world does not even know I'm alive. *Advice to Self* – *Stick with those people you like and get along with. Leave others alone. Just observe others and don't judge them, categorize them, or in any way get in their way – unless you want to or need to. Minimize contact with those you don't get along with or you don't like. Don't let you (yourself) and/or others get you down. Keep your self-esteem and don't let anyone bully you. Stick with other people who treat you with respect and you feel good around. Trust your own intuition to guide you as to who to "hang around with" and those to avoid. Everyone in the world does not have to like you, Tom, and don't try to get others to like you. Let mutual attraction take place. Realize that there are not many who are like you and that's okay. It's okay to have a few good friends and family members – instead of many. Move on in your life now, Tom, with less stress, since you're not responsible for everyone and everything. You don't have to fix everyone and everything, too.*

I'm me and I can vote based on what reflects me – it's my right as a U.S. citizen. I'm not competitive – it means more to get along with others, than to be number one, the best, or the greatest. I like quiet conversations that make sense to me – I dislike loud abrasive people who don't make sense to me, tell lies, cheat in life to just get ahead, bully others, etc. I like to check out each candidate and judge them by their previous actions more so than their words/promises. If a candidate fits me, then I vote for them. Sometimes, I vote for the person who I think will do the least harm, however, picking the best of the bunch. _Advice to Self – Vote and be done with it!_

Before the pandemic, I frequently went to my local YMCA™'s, especially to take the Step Aerobics Classes. At the height of the pandemic, the Y's, along with other health facilities were closed, as they were deemed non-essential. It is now 2022 and all health clubs are open now, unless some went out of business because of the pandemic or other reasons. I think it's quieter now in the Y's near me and have fewer people now – but it is getting better. I miss the "camaraderie" conversations in the locker rooms – as I said it seems more subdued and people seem to keep to themselves more. Maybe we just got used to being alone, by ourselves. I most certainly do not miss the political discussions that would go on in the locker rooms, though, now. Yes, I chimed in years past, but I'm done doing that anymore. I don't want to get all wound up again, like I used to, and accomplish no useful purpose at all – just a bunch of guys venting, often quite heated. Yes, I do hear the political conversations starting again, but I also hear others like me who learned their lesson and just don't want to get involved in those discussions anymore. By the way, Step Aerobics is no longer offered near me in person. I miss that but several classes were canceled or eliminated when health clubs reopened after the pandemic. Oh well, I still get a good workout doing something else. I'm just glad to have what I have. I want to stay healthy – physically, mentally, and emotionally.

Okay, maybe I was an Emotional "Long-Hauler" when I first started this chapter, hacking up "emotional hairballs" of what happened over the last few years – but I feel better now. I'm not stuck anymore. I've got a few more things to write in this chapter but I think I'm almost done. I wrote what happened and how I felt/feel about it – and as I write, I'm developing an "action plan" on how I'd like to handle "what's probably going to happen again, especially with politics".

One of the therapists I went to some time ago, advised me to just observe, rather than judge people or events. I did pretty good for a while in doing this, but with the events of the last few years, I "fell off the wagon" and relapsed into my old judging habits. Frequently, I misjudge people or situations. This type of thinking does me no good and especially when I "advise" people on what they should or should not do. *Advice to Self – Going forward, try harder to live your own life and let others live their lives the way they want to. Let others be, who irritate you. Shift your thinking Tom to something else. Don't mentally try to figure out what kind of person they are, to categorize them, to mentally label them. This is not good for you. Stay out of others' way, Tom. Let them be. In most cases, you're not responsible for them. If something comes up, then deal with it. Be open-minded and try to take people and events at face value. Don't imagine things that aren't there. Don't make something out of nothing. And, yes, stay away from the news.*

I wore myself out over the last few years with politics and the pandemic, trying to make sense of what I was hearing and seeing. Maybe that's just how my brain is "wired". What happens around me is processed in my brain based on what happened before, I think. Making sense of things has served me well in life up until the last few years. Maybe everyone does it. Well, I got "overloaded", especially with misinformation and/or conflicting information. Yikes – crazy making!! As far as health matters, I finally "got out of the mental weeds" and just relied on my own personal doctor to advise me/us what to do and not do with Covid – just like he had done for many other health matters. As far as making sense of politics, I just gave up. With local/world events, I try to be aware and care, but again many local/world events just don't make sense to me. With the economy, it does me no good at all to worry – going forward I want to continue to "live within our means", adjusting as needed depending on inflation, recessions, economic depressions, etc. In essence, "take life as it comes" and not worry so much about the future. If I have financial concerns, I can get good advice from my financial counselor on what to do and not do, as events come up. *Advice to Self – When mentally overloaded, stop right there and limit information input. Relax. Seek "good information" from those you trust, asking their advice on what to do or not do. With good information, decide then what to do or not do. Try not to react, Tom, impulsively, going off "halfcocked". Take your time and make good decisions based on good information and your own internal intuition.*

It's now September 2022 and people don't talk much about the Pandemic anymore. Maybe others didn't think it was much of a deal. It seemed important to me – a once in a lifetime (probably) event. About the only ones concerned with Covid are those whose health is not so good to begin with and they have to take special precautions. Troubling Local/World Events are probably going to happen again, sometime soon. Political talk/news is at a lull now, but will probably heat up in the future. The next presidential election is in 2024 and that's going to be a big one, I'm sure. <u>*Advice to Self*</u> – *Stay on course by not chasing the news, Tom. Since detaching from the news, my quality of life and stress level have greatly improved. If something comes up, deal with it then. For now, "Stay Calm and Carry On", just like the book I mentioned earlier in my story.*

I started this book about a year ago now in November of 2021 using a speech-to-text app on my phone. It's October 2022 now and I see I've been working on this book for a year now – a little bit at a time. I'm getting tired of working so hard on this book and am anxious to move on to my next book(s). In 2021, I got a bunch of books at the library on how the Pandemic was affecting people, but none considered the whole picture around the Pandemic involving Politics and other life events. I learned a lot from these early books and they reminded me of how events affected me and us personally – and I wrote about them in this book. Just writing this book, I feel happier, stronger, and healthier – it must be working – at least for me – I hope whoever reads this will find benefit in my writing in their own lives. Today, I have great hope for my life and the lives of others, which I did not have over the last few years – I guess this relates to the song "Let There Be Peace on Earth, and Let It Begin with Me" by Sy Miller and Jill Jackson, 1955. There is hope, and let it begin with me – the only person I can truly control.

As I said, it's now 2022 and I got another bunch of books at the library about "What just happened?" – Pandemic, politics, etc. By the way what we all went through was very similar to what happened in the 1918 Flu Epidemic with politics, people doing whatever they wanted, economic effects, etc. I didn't know that until I found some references on this, maybe from another book I wrote during the pandemic – if interested, let me know and I can dig up those references. If you're thinking of telling your own story, maybe you also want to get some books, articles, songs, pictures, etc. to give you some writing prompts. In this book, I also list later some writing prompts for you to expand on personally.

What a touching story "Our bodies stay home, our imaginations run free : a Coronavirus COVID-19 story for children" by Lora L. Hyler is! It described a child going through the Pandemic – the sadness, the fears, the isolation, etc. that I also felt during that time. It is also a book of hope. During the pandemic, I saw pictures of how healthcare workers dressed from head to toe, totally covered, and imagined how hard and scary this must have been for children and infants requiring healthcare at that time. Wow!

"Leading through a pandemic : the inside story of humanity, innovation, and lessons learned during the Covid-19 crisis" by Michael J. Dowling et. al. shows how many healthcare workers survived, and some who didn't, in the pandemic. I think the psychological and emotional toll is still unfolding for many, as well as the prolonged physical effects of Covid, e.g. long-haulers, etc. I could just imagine as events unfolded how essential workers must have felt, some even isolating from their families. Wow, again. Maybe future stories will reveal later the effects of PTSD, much like the aftereffects of 9/11 here in the U.S. I'm writing this book for anyone interested and also those who are still hurting. I hope my work will help someone, somewhere, sometime.

There were many books written about the Pandemic, Politics, etc. over the last few years. Many of these books just recited statistics, events, timelines, results, effects, future planning, etc. These kinds of books were not of interest to me in writing my book. I was interested in books and stories that described the personal lives of people at the time. Also, books that showed pictures of people reminded me of how I felt at that time – or I could imagine how those people were when the pictures were taken. One book that really touched me was "COVID chronicles : true stories from the front lines of COVID-19" by Ethan Sacks et. al. I teared up just seeing the pictures and words - What all did we go through! – Some more than others. We're all just glad to be alive and healthy today telling our stories.

On the flip side, I also liked seeing how people got on with life at that time. One unique book that I liked was "Safer at home in Waupaca : recipes and stories from our community during the pandemic" by the Waupaca Historical Society. Interesting. Another shows how parents coped, at least Moms, in the book "Moms don't have time to have kids : a timeless anthology" by Zibby Owens et. al. As I'm writing this, I don't think I saw any books on how fathers and men, in general, coped during the pandemic. Maybe this is also a possible future book for someone. Maybe I'm the only man, father, or grandfather – so far- who has written about what I went through, and what we all went through. Men have feelings, too, I'd like to say. Sometimes we don't show it openly, but many men do. I think it's best to just let it out – like I'm doing in this book.

Here it is 2022 – this writing must be helping! I'm much less dependent on the news and much less Germaphobic! I don't talk or even think much about the pandemic, politics, etc. Yes, I am still troubled by local/world events and the economy, as they happen – but realize there is not much I can do about much of anything – except to live the best life I can, try to be as independent (self-responsible) as I can as an older person – be happy and healthy – and appreciate life, as it is. It could be worse, you betcha! I'm a lucky person and want to keep that kind of thinking, moving forward.

I'm writing this paragraph in the present (2022) – talking about unity and the opposite – division. I've never seen so much division of people. I think years ago, the big dividers of people were politics, religion, race, ethnicity, status in life, wealth or lack thereof, etc. Now, in these last few years, we can add people divided on how health should be managed. I think years ago, we pretty well left that up to our doctors to give us good advice – which we either followed or not. Over the last few years, it seems like everyone, including politicians and religious leaders, have an opinion on how the pandemic, and health in general, should be managed. Politics, religion, masking, vaccinations, etc. have actually divided families, friends, in fact I think the whole United States. From what I see, it's like navigating a minefield of what to talk about these days. I'm actually afraid to say anything. I think there are quite a few angry and dangerous people out there – and I'm afraid to set them off. Wow. Too bad. I don't know the answer except for myself and my family – stay safe and healthy – as best as we can.

During the pandemic, there sure was division in government and even individuals on what to do and how to do it. Some politicians seemingly wanted to sacrifice the health of the people to keep the economy going. On the flip side, other politicians wanted to place the health of the country first and deal with the economic fallout, as it happened. Whatever health guidelines, even mandatory, were soon circumvented, by either politicians or individuals. Yes, mandatory guidelines were in place, but many individuals just ignored them. Furthermore, police officials just said outright they weren't going to enforce the guidelines. I think at one time, here in Wisconsin, there was a $200 penalty, the news of which soon faded into obscurity. Recently, we visited a gift shop and I casually talked to an employee asking how they survived the pandemic. The answer was that the owner checked to see what it would take to be deemed "essential" and did that – they added a few food items, and then they were able to re-open! Wow, all this just baffles me how we even survived the Covid attack. I wonder what would happen if other big events were to happen and everyone just did their own thing???? I also wondered during that time how difficult it must have been for government leaders to choose between the health and survival of people vs. the economy – what a knife-edge balance that must have been for some – and a highly emotional moral decision for some – at least it would have been for me, if I was in office.

What brought hope for me one day, during the dark times of the pandemic for me, was listening to the theme music from Star Wars™. I like the concept of "Trust the Force". I like hope. I thrive on hope. Hope switches me from negativity to positivity. Hearing this reminded me of the movie, which I liked so much, too – got my mind off myself, my day, and my life – as it was during those times. Maybe I thought "trusting the force" was trusting my own self – my inner self - in a time of such indecision by others.

It bothered me, too, how people were treated for Covid based on their wealth, their status, their color, their sex, their background, etc. There was indeed a discrepancy in how people, in general, received healthcare – but, alas, that is nothing new – it just was more apparent to me listening to the news and other broadcasts related to Covid. I also realized how lucky I, and we, are to be living in a developed country with good healthcare, compared to the other 90% of the population of the earth.

There were some books written or prepared to help children cope with those hard times. I don't know if there were similar books in the 1918 flu time, but maybe this could be an idea for a book for someone to follow up on. The books and activities I saw were hard copy books, eBooks, activity/drawing books, apps on phones, videos, etc. I liked the book "What kids did : stories of kindness and invention in the time of COVID-19" by Erin Silver. This book showed me the resilience of kids, which I kind of would like more of. Some books showed how kids found comfort in other family members, e.g. grandparents, when parents were so busy trying to make ends meet and coping with life after job losses, illness, death, etc. Some books showed how kids, and adults, made the best of masking – decorating their masks with smiles and other creations. I saw some doctors had a picture showing their faces underneath all the protective garb – just to show, particularly children, that there was a caring person inside the scary costume. Another book I liked that showed resilience is "Sunny days inside and other stories" by Caroline Adderson. Some books were written to help young children understand what was going on in their little world, in their family, at their school, why they can't play like they used to do, to explain why everyone is acting so weird – wearing masks and standing so far away, why grandma can't hug them, etc. One book like this is "Zen Pig. Book 9, Distance, masks & kindness" by Mark Brown.

The Pandemic was a game-changer for all of us in one way or another. As I said before, for me, it was a mix of politics, the pandemic, and others. We did, and still do, hear of how the pandemic affected others. Just today, I saw on Facebook™ that the U.S. Surgeon General is concerned about the effect the pandemic had on mental health – and it is still unfolding – much like PTSD, after the event. Anyhow, this is one reason I'm writing this book, explaining how I coped, am coping, and am making a game plan for the future. The book "The year that changed our world" by Marielle Eudes et. al. encapsulates in photographs of what happened in the Covid-19 in just one year. You should get this book if you want to review "what just happened". Seeing those pictures made me cry. Such losses. I'm amazed we all came through it, as well as we did. I love how this book covers the world instead of just the U.S. where I live. How can we not remember what happened, what is happening now, and what will probably happen again in the future? At least some people are writing and making other creative works for others to find in the future – like making a time capsule. Maybe we can learn from this....or not. Where I live, I hear very little about the pandemic these days in 2022. It's like it's forgotten. Maybe it is, but I still remember and am affected.

Here are a few more anomalies of pandemic life, but I'm going to end here. I and everyone could go on forever with memories, but I'm not. Maybe others want to write their own books. Anyhow, story time – I was riding my bicycle passing a church with a long line of cars in the parking lot. I was puzzled and am a very curious person. I asked someone, at a distance, of course. The person replied that the people in the cars were getting "drive-through communion". Wow, I thought. I could see those giving communion were all garbed up for personal protection and gave little packages of a wafer and wine/juice – prepackaged. Amazing, I thought. Another thing that surprised me is how the National Guard helped out with Covid healthcare in various ways – though I'm not sure how much training they had to do so. Okay, I'm ending writing my "pandemic memoirs". I still have them, of course, and will always have them, but I want to move on in my own "New Normal", enjoying life. Whoever reads this, if anyone, I wish you well.

Somewhere earlier I said I coped by walking and listening to audiobooks. I picked what was available at the time and one I heard was related to "Chicken Soup for the Soul™" stories. I found these inspirational and many times, I just stopped walking and cried – then I kept walking. Anyhow, I think I remember one audio that talked of how the pandemic got them to do something with "Chicken Soup for the Soul™" – maybe I'm wrong though. What I heard then is a blur now. Just recently I picked up the book "Chicken soup for the soul : tough times won't last, but tough people will : 101 stories about overcoming life's challenges" by Amy Newmark (Compiler). Excellent book of Pandemic related stories.

Things have settled down now in November of 2022. The midterm elections seemed to be calmer, by far, than 2020. The Pandemic is pretty well over, at least the physical aspects of it. We now have inflation and maybe an upcoming recession, but that happens now and then. Life is good now for many people, including me. The years 2015-2022 have been a learning lesson for me. I saw, heard, and experienced so much.

I'm writing about my experiences to help myself and maybe others. Yes, things are better now, but I'm still glad I wrote all this, at least to help myself in the future in case of political turmoil, pandemics, economic downturns, or just plain life events. My writing gives me a plan of action going forward.

This is the final paragraph of My Story. I've got to end sometime and this is a good time to just stop. If you want more of my pandemic memories let me know, but I'm sure you all have stories of your own. I feel like "I'm done" processing all "what just happened, what is happening now, and what is probably going to happen in the future again". My stress level is very good now as a result of my journaling (writing) this chapter and this book. I'm healed! – well, maybe not completely. The memories are still with me, the emotions have been resolved, and I have a good plan for now and in the future. This is how journaling helps me. I've used writing/journaling a lot in my life to "sort things out". I start my morning with a God Letter, which seems to give me comfort and guidance for my day ahead. When something comes up I talk it out and write it out, if need be. Sometimes, I even sketch things out, making flow charts, scrapbooks, etc. to help me "get my head around" what's going on in my life. I don't "bottle things up" anymore. That is what got me sick many years ago. Everyone is different and handles life differently. I've shown you "How to Journal Through Tough Times" by showing you My Story in this book. I hope my work helps you and or others in some way. If you do decide to write your "Pandemic Memoirs" and want to share them with others, check with your local library on where you can add your story to others' stories. At the time of this writing, I couldn't find a single depository of pandemic stories worldwide, but maybe in years to come someone will create such a thing.

Writing Prompts for You

WHATEVER WRITING PROMPT below causes you to react emotionally is what you probably should write about. There might be more than one topic that does so, but just keep on writing. What do you have to lose? You might find just what you're looking for.

If you have serious issues, <u>please please</u> seek out professional help, as I did. They are specially trained to help people overcome the Tough Times in a person's present or past. Don't let it get you down. If the feelings are too intense in your journaling, go get some help before it gets "out of hand". You want to get better and stay better, just as I do. Journaling does help most people process things, but it does not take the place of therapy or the like.

Later in this chapter, I give you writing prompts for the Pandemic, Politics, Economy, etc., but first I'd like to give you some Internet Search String Examples of how to find prompts just for what is troubling you now.

(writing OR journaling) prompts tough times
(writing OR journaling) prompts (sickness OR disability)
(writing OR journaling) prompts (grieving OR loss OR sad)
(writing OR journaling) prompts (debt OR recession)
(writing OR journaling) prompts (fear OR anxiety)
(writing OR journaling) prompts depression
(writing OR journaling) prompts (anger OR resentment OR frustration)
(writing OR journaling) prompts stress
(writing OR journaling) prompts cancer
(writing OR journaling) prompts (shame OR guilt)

(writing OR journaling) prompts hurt
(writing OR journaling) prompts struggling
(writing OR journaling) prompts relapse
(writing OR journaling) prompts relationships
(writing OR journaling) prompts pain
(writing OR journaling) prompts (gratitude OR thankful)

These are just examples – you can modify as needed to get the words flowing from your "insides" to your "outside", where you can see what's really going on. For example, if you are all upset about a breakup with someone you could search for *(writing OR journaling) prompts breakups* – and go from there.

If you want to know more about journaling, in general, check with your local library. They might have some good suggestions for you – books, local events, journaling clubs, courses, tools, etc.

Also, here's an Internet Search String you can use on your own to find more information, products, clubs, etc. on journaling, too.

(writing OR journaling) (journals OR notebooks OR diaries OR workbooks)

<u>Related to "My Story", here are some prompts for you to consider.</u>

1. What bothered you most in the last few years? Pandemic? Politics? Economy? Events?
2. Were you on the "Front Lines" somewhere in the last few years? Pandemic? Political Turmoil? Tragic Events?
3. How did you get through the Pandemic, Politics, and Events these last years?
4. Who or What helped you the most in surviving the recent events?
5. What would you do differently next time around?
6. What carryover "Yuck" do you want to get rid of moving

forward?

7. At your age, how did the recent events affect you?
8. Where did you get your news from? Was it helpful to you? How did you react to the unfolding news each day, each hour, each minute?
9. Did you learn anything from past pandemics, past political turmoils, past economic situations, and past world/local events?
10. How did you make sense out of all that was happening?
11. Did you ever live through similar times in your life?
12. How was your work, and life, in general, affected in recent years?
13. What did you do to stay active, to stay sane, when you couldn't do what you wanted to do?
14. Did you have any health problems during the pandemic or because of the pandemic? Stress-related, do you think?
15. What words would you describe the last few years?
16. What emotions did you have as time went along?
17. What did you have too much of and too little of over the past few years?
18. Did you miss something or someone during the pandemic?
19. What good happened? What bad happened?
20. What new activities did you do during the pandemic? What did you give up? What did you go back to, now?
21. Did you or do you find comfort in religion or something else?
22. What happened to your support system during the pandemic? How did you cope?
23. Did you struggle with depression or other health conditions then? Now?
24. What activities did you do when quarantined? outside? Inside?
25. Did you work during the pandemic? How did you feel doing so?

26. Did you work from home more? What about now?
27. Are you a "Long-Hauler" with lingering Covid after-effects?
28. Do you think you lost part of your life over the last few years?
29. How did the Elections affect you? Are you worried about the future?
30. Did the Events at the White House on January 6 bother you? If so, how?
31. Did you ever think there would be an event like the Pandemic to affect your life so drastically?
32. Did you have a premonition something adverse was going to happen?
33. How did you cope with the shortages, hoarding, and supply chain problems, etc?
34. Did you find ways around situations, e.g. make your own masks, hand sanitizer, etc?
35. Have you ever been in a global situation – something that affected the whole world before?
36. How did the events affect you as a senior citizen, young person, parent, compromised immune system person, etc.?
37. Were you retired then? How did/do events affect you then or now?
38. How did the slow lifestyle affect you when we were in lockdown?
39. Were you lonely at any time then? Now?
40. Were you in a nursing home – or did you know of someone who was? What happened?
41. How did you make-do with family/friends contact? Phone? ZOOM™? Meet outside?
42. Were you afraid to touch anything or maybe even breathe? What about now?
43. Did you become afraid of people, either due to the pandemic or volatile conditions around politics or something else?

44. Were you angry about what people did or didn't do during the pandemic or political situations?

45. Were you suspicious of the various Covid remedies proposed, even the vaccines?

46. Are you getting tired of being vaccinated/boosted or following "guidelines"?

47. Did you feel helpless at any time? What about now?

48. Was everything closed around you? What was open?

49. How did you cut your hair and deal with the closing of other non-essential services?

50. How did social media affect you?

51. Whom did you trust during the pandemic or political situations?

52. Did you think this was real?

53. Did you think some/most of the news was fake? What about now?

54. What did you think of the government then? What about now? Can you do anything about it?

55. Did you watch TV, movies, and use the Internet more? Did you get tired of doing the same-old, same-old?

56. How did you have contact with people during the pandemic? Were you cautious? Why?

57. Do you think the country is divided? How does this affect you personally? Are you afraid of the future? How so?

58. Did you look for the good each day or did life get you down? What about now?

59. Do you think you have PTSD as a result of "what just happened, what is still happening, and what will probably happen again"?

60. Did you need help during the pandemic? How did that make you feel?

61. What do you have a new appreciation of now?

62. Did you read more or journal more? What else did you do?
63. Are you continuing your past pandemic activities or are you going back to what you did before the pandemic?
64. Do you miss anything from the pandemic? What?
65. Do you regret something you did or didn't do?
66. Remember when all playground equipment was covered with tape during lockdown? How did this affect you?
67. Do you sense the tension these days?
68. Are you afraid to say anything about politics these days?...or about any of the "touchy" topics that might anger someone?
69. What good did you do to make things a little better? What are you proud of?
70. Did you feel like you were in a "black hole"?...how about now?
71. Did you feel trapped?...how about now?
72. What innovations did you and/or others have to make?
73. Did you overwork during the pandemic?....underwork?...out of work?
74. How has your social circle changed due to recent events?
75. Did you sometimes feel like just a number?...number of those sick?...number of those unemployed?...number of those who can or cannot be vaccinated?
76. Who, in power, bothered you the most then?...how about now?
77. Were you bored to death? What did you do about it?...or not do about it?
78. How did other countries' troubles affect you? How about now?
79. Were you homeless?...or near so?...what changed?
80. Did you feel sorry for others? Did you try to do something about it? What was their reaction?
81. What do you think will happen now? Can you do anything about it? What do you fear the most?

82. Are you LBGQT? What happened to you in the last few years?

83. Whom do you trust now? There must be someone.

84. What's next with Covid? Politics? The Economy? Who knows? Can you plan for anything or not?

85. Are you in a state of turmoil now? Were you then? What made it better for you?

86. What was the most terrible thing you went through, saw, or heard about?

87. What do you need to "work through" now to move ahead? Do you need help doing so?

88. Do you feel stuck now?...not knowing what to do next? Can you do anything at all to improve your "lot in life"? One small thing? Try it.

89. Did you profit from these last few years? How do you feel about others who did?

90. Can you move on with your life now? Can you make a new life? Do you have to?

91. Is everything getting out of your price range? What are you doing about it? Is what you're doing the best thing to do, long-term?

92. Did you feel like a "prisoner" in your own house? What happened when you did go out?

93. Did the pandemic affect your pets and/or farm animals in any way?

94. Could you find everything you needed to live? Did you have to cut back on something? What about now?

95. Are you trying to catch up now, trying to retrieve your losses?

96. During the pandemic, were you a healthcare worker? How did this affect you? Do you need help with PTSD?

97. Are you concerned about the level of violence near you or in the world now? Is there anything you can do about it?

98. Are you or were you a law enforcement worker? What changes have you seen over the last few years? How did it affect you? Now?

99. Where did you see unity these last few years?...people helping people...joining together for good?

100. Where do you see hope these days? Can others see hope in you?

101. How have things gotten better?....worse?

102. Were you or are you incarcerated, bed-bound, or confined in a nursing home? How did the last years affect you? Now?

103. Where do you go for relief now and over the last few years? How is it working out for you?

104. Did you use unhealthy means to cope with life then? Now? Gain weight? Use drugs/alcohol? Smoke more?

105. Does what happened bother you or are you just able to "shrug it off"?

106. Did you "bury emotions" during the last years or anytime in your life? Are they bothering you to the point of doing something about it?

107. Have you been "holding back" tears or other means of grieving?

108. What decisions have you made due to the pandemic, politics, economy, and local/world events?

109. Did you try to make sense of things then? Now?

110. How much did you listen to the news then? What about now?

111. Did you realize how fragile life is?...as well as the world around you?

112. Did you put your life on hold then? What about now? What are you waiting for?

113. What news bothers you the most? – Politics, Covid, Current Events, or the Economy?

114. Is there anything you can do about what happens politically,

except to vote and encourage others to also vote?

115. Why do you listen to the news so much, when it bothers you so much?

116. Do you realize that you mostly hear bad news? How do you feel inside when you listen, and maybe dwell, on bad news?

117. How did the shootings, wars, and other violence affect you?

118. Do you think what happened and/or what is happening now is fair and just?

119. What did you expect from politics and politicians then? Now? Were your expectations realistic?

120. What do you think of our government on an emotional level? Can you do anything about it?

121. Does it help to complain and/or worry about what just happened...what is happening now...and what might happen?

122. Can you create and live within your own world, despite what goes on around you? How could you do this?

123. Have you ever tried to look for the good?

124. What about the rest of the world?...the planet?...living creatures other than us humans?

125. Can you accept, for your own sake, what others do or don't do?

126. Why do you let "it" or "them" bother you so much? What can you do to lessen troubling situations that bother you?

127. Can you find someone worse off than you and realize how good you have it?

128. What peace and happiness can you find in your life today?

129. What can you do to make the world a better place? Can you start now?

130. Why "stick around" situations, people, or events that bother you? Got any ideas on how to improve your life?

131. Are you affected by racism/prejudice or other judging? Is there anything you can do about it?

132. Are you letting the past affect your life today?

133. Can you move on now? What's holding you back?
134. How has your opinion changed on anything or anyone as a result of these last few years?
135. Did you think things were finally resolved only to have it change for the worse again?
136. Are you so sick of wearing masks and other Covid prevention methods?
137. What's happened to your health, physically and/or mentally over the last few years?
138. Did what happened trigger adverse memories from your past?
139. If you can't do anything except vote, and encourage others to vote, why get all worked up about what's going on politically?
140. Are current politics and politicians adversely affecting your health?
141. Are current politics and politicians stressing you out more than you can handle?
142. What or who helped you cope over the last few years?
143. What bothered you the most – pandemic, politics, or something else?
144. Who and What do you want in <u>YOUR</u> "New Normal"?
145. What will it take for you to move on in your life?
146. What are your fears for the future?
147. Do you think the worst is over?
148. Were you bullied during the Pandemic? Made fun of?
149. Are you, or did you, let fear drive you over the last few years?
150. Are we as a country making progress?
151. Were you afraid of becoming sick with Covid, being hospitalized, and/or dying alone?
152. Did the isolation bother you? – Or were you relieved to have an excuse not to be with people?
153. Do you have any lingering effects of the pandemic, political turmoil, local/world events, and/or the economy? If so, how

are you dealing or coping with these remnants of the last few years?

154. Did you miss the touch of other people? – Intimacy, hugging, handshaking, brushing by others casually.

155. What did you do for exercise during the pandemic, lockdown, quarantining, and closings?

156. Did you hold your breath, turn your head, or avoid others during Covid? Do you still find yourself doing this?

157. How did you interact with the "outside world" when everything was closed and we couldn't be around each other safely?

158. What or who did you lose in the Pandemic, or even the Economy now?

159. Were you in an area where literally "everything stopped"?

160. Do you feel like you're in danger now, going out and about?

161. Did you gain anything during the Pandemic?

162. How are you doing with the current Inflation? Do you fear a recession/depression?

163. What has changed since the Pandemic?

164. Did you learn anything over the last few years with all that went on?

165. How did you find relief from stress?

166. Were you surprised at anything that went on? Pleasantly? Or Not?

167. What self-care or coping strategies are you going to use in YOUR "New Normal" now?

168. Are you having trouble moving on? Are you stuck?

169. What did you learn about people generally with all this upheaval?

170. Were you a shift worker and had a hard time?

171. What's next for you?

172. What are your biggest memories of "What Just Happened"?

173. How has your gender preference affected you over the last few years?

174. Did your race, looks, or anything else affect your life more over the last few years?

175. What was it like being in the "high-risk" category during the Pandemic? Now?

176. Who have you had to say "GoodBye" to?

177. What do you miss now the most?

178. Were your animals or pets affected by what happened these last few years?

179. What hard decisions did you have to make?

180. What kept you going in the hard times?

181. Did you have any adventures during all the troubles?

182. Did you vote? If not, why not?

183. Do you really think worrying about the outcomes of elections helps you?

184. What is your passion going forward in life?

185. Have your "bad habits" gotten better or worse over the last few years?

186. What mischief did you or others get into while everything was going on?

187. What are you going to tell your "future generations" about what just happened?

188. What would you like to tell your "future self"?

189. Are you "sick and tired" of everything? (Please watch yourself for depression and get help if you need to.)

190. As a teen or child, how are you feeling now as a result of all that's happened?

191. What do you need to "pour your heart out" on now?

192. What goals do you have for the future now?

193. Who inspires you?

194. Do you need/want to make changes in your social media

interaction going forward?

195. How has violence affected you?
196. What do you need to move on now?
197. How are you going to handle misinformation in the future?
198. Have your priorities changed now?
199. What are you going to do with YOUR "Wake Up Call" that just happened?
200. What frightened you the most?
201. What "action plan" do you have moving forward?
202. How did being incarcerated affect you during that time?
203. What do you think and feel about the school shootings that went on?
204. What are your feelings about gun controls?
205. How has all this political turmoil affected you?
206. How are you managing money now?
207. Are you unemployed due to what just happened?
208. What are you going to do about all this stress in your life?
209. Are you using way too much credit just to get by these days?
210. Do you worry about how all this is affecting your children and grandchildren?
211. What has worked before that you're not doing now?
212. Do you need more of something to manage these days?
213. Is there anything you can do now to improve your situation?
214. How has terrorism, or even bullying, affected you?
215. Did technology help you "get by"?
216. How were you affected in your relationships these last few years?
217. What did you use to amuse yourself during quarantine or lockdown?
218. Do you see your life getting better or getting worse?
219. Can you manage as a parent, caregiver, or anything else?
220. If you're writing as a child or teen, how has all this affected

you?

221. Can you talk to someone about all your anxiety?
222. Do you find comfort in *nature*?
223. What did you lose and/or gain over all this?
224. What do you think of the country where you live?
225. How does all this make you feel?
226. What worries you the most right now?
227. What do you do for comfort in troubled times?
228. What do you still need to resolve in your life now?
229. How have your beliefs changed because of recent events?
230. How have you grown as a result of what just happened?
231. What are you still holding on to?
232. What good things can you fill your mind with?
233. Which doors are closed to you now? Which are open?
234. Can you move toward the open doors in your life?
235. What's holding you back now?
236. What do you have to look forward to now?
237. What is your life mission?
238. What keeps you going?
239. What can you do today to "have a good day"?
240. Can you just let others be and live your own life?
241. What "silver lining" do you see in your present circumstance?
242. Is it <u>all</u> bad? What's good about it?
243. What can you do for fun today...to lighten up?
244. What healthy things make you feel good?
245. What can you do with what you've got to work with?
246. Can you break it down into more manageable chunks?
247. How can you make someone feel good about themselves?
248. What physical action can you do to symbolize your "letting go"?
249. What are you grateful and thankful for?
250. What is YOUR "*<u>Advice to Self</u>*" going forward?

Conclusion

PONDERING IS GOOD, but sometimes I've found it necessary to "unponder" what's going on – to break it down into more manageable pieces. As you learned in this book, I write, amongst other means to "sort it out" or to "sort myself out". I showed you how I do it and maybe you want to do something similar (or not). Right now, I'm getting on with my life. How about you?

The End (of this book)

Thanks to Canva[1] for the wonderful Design Tool, my Publishers, Microsoft Word, my Personal Life Experiences, the Universe for providing Information and Guidance in writing this book, and most importantly to you for reading this book.

Tom Garz - TG Ideas LLC[2]
691 S. Green Bay Rd. # 180
Neenah, WI 54956 U.S.A.
E-Mail tgideas@gmail.com

---

1. https://www.canva.com/

2. https://sites.google.com/site/tgideas/

accident, or any other means. Additional Disclaimers are at https://sites.google.com/site/tgideas/ideas-for-products-or-services/disclaimer

Don't miss out!

Visit the website below and you can sign up to receive emails whenever Tom Garz publishes a new book. There's no charge and no obligation.

https://books2read.com/r/B-A-BDUH-FTEDC

BOOKS 2 READ

Connecting independent readers to independent writers.

Also by Tom Garz

Paging Dr. Within: How to Become, Be, and/or Make a "Patient Listener" and/or a "Super Symptom Checker"
Coronavirus-The Inside Story: Multidimensional Prevention and Treatment
Living Through This Pandemic: "Just for Today"
Over 700 Ways to Live "Just for Today"
How to Journal Through Tough Times

About the Author

I write because this is something I can do. I wrote as a boy because I stuttered so badly I couldn't even say my own name.

Through time, writing has served me well in my life and career. I worked as a Technical Writer for some time. Later, as an Engineer, I wrote up a "Theory of Operation" from which multiple machines were built. I had an "Ideas for Products or Services Newsletter" for a short time. I started Blogging in 2003 and now have several Blogs.

Shortly before the Pandemic, I decided to write books since I couldn't find a job that fit me in "retirement". Now I'm quite content that writing gives me a sense of purpose, leaves a legacy, and gives me a voice of what's inside of me.

For many years, I have privately journaled. Now in my books, I "publicly journal" to help myself and others.

Most of my current books are for those who are hurting in some way. My books, so far, do indeed reflect me and my history. I've been around sickness all my life – either my own or with family members. Perhaps my books might help people "get better and stay better".

I try to provide encouragement, hope, and maybe some ideas on how to think or act better – never medical advice, just information.

I hope my Guided Journals give people a way to "sort themselves out", like I do.

My first and favorite book is Paging Dr. Within.

Sometimes I write technically and sometimes I write from my heart.

The greatest challenge in me writing is actually doing it. Writing was easier during the Pandemic when there was nothing much else to do.

Writing helped preserve my sanity during the Pandemic, though some might say differently. :-)

About the Publisher

TG Ideas LLC is a limited liability company registered in Wisconsin. It was formed in Spring of 2003.

The Mission of TG Ideas LLC is to "Help make this a better world by providing information to others on what has been done already and offer up ideas on what else might be done"

TG Ideas does not make or sell any products, other than publications.

Contact - tgideas@gmail.com

www.ingramcontent.com/pod-product-compliance
Lightning Source LLC
Chambersburg PA
CBHW021746150726
47989CB00004B/1533